A. Dumbledog and *Emily Carding*

SIMPLE WISDOM *of the* HOUSEHOLD DOG

An Oracle

4880 Lower Valley Road • Atglen, PA 19310

Other Schiffer Books By The Author:
The Transparent Tarot   978-0-7643-3003-2 $59.99
The Transparent Oracle   978-0-7643-3486-3 $39.99
Tarot of the Sidhe   978-0-7643-3599-0 $24.99

Copyright © 2012 by Emily Carding
Library of Congress Control Number: 2012940617

All rights reserved. No part of this work may be reproduced or used in any form or by any means—graphic, electronic, or mechanical, including photocopying or information storage and retrieval systems—without written permission from the publisher.

The scanning, uploading and distribution of this book or any part thereof via the Internet or via any other means without the permission of the publisher is illegal and punishable by law. Please purchase only authorized editions and do not participate in or encourage the electronic piracy of copyrighted materials.

"Schiffer," "Schiffer Publishing Ltd. & Design," and the "Design of pen and inkwell" are registered trademarks of Schiffer Publishing Ltd.

Designed by RoS
Type set in Trajan Pro/Garamond
ISBN: 978-0-7643-4135-9

Printed in China

Schiffer Books are available at special discounts for bulk purchases for sales promotions or premiums. Special editions, including personalized covers, corporate imprints, and excerpts can be created in large quantities for special needs. For more information contact the publisher:

Published by Schiffer Publishing Ltd.
4880 Lower Valley Road
Atglen, PA 19310
Phone: (610) 593-1777; Fax: (610) 593-2002
E-mail: Info@schifferbooks.com

For the largest selection of fine reference books on this and related subjects, please visit our website at
www.schifferbooks.com
We are always looking for people to write books on new and related subjects. If you have an idea for a book, please contact us at
proposals@schifferbooks.com

This book may be purchased from the publisher.
Please try your bookstore first.
You may write for a free catalog.

In Europe, Schiffer books are distributed by
Bushwood Books
6 Marksbury Ave.
Kew Gardens
Surrey TW9 4JF England
Phone: 44 (0) 20 8392 8585; Fax: 44 (0) 20 8392 9876
E-mail: info@bushwoodbooks.co.uk
Website: www.bushwoodbooks.co.uk

DEDICATION

Albus and Emily would both like to dedicate this work to one very special Bear, who they both love very much indeed and without whom this deck would never have happened.

Acknowledgments

Albus and I would both like to thank everyone who has been so supportive of our work. We would particularly like to mention my husband, Jules, for incredible support, humour, and inspiration, and Willow for being such a splendid fairy model. Huge thanks as always to Dinah, Pete, and everyone at Schiffer Publishing, LTD for having faith in another one of my projects! I also give much love and thanks to Barbara Moore for a generous and touching Foreword.

Thank you Kether Kitty for proofreading and being the perfect Nemesis, and to the other Catballah Cats of the Supurrrnal Triad, Chokmah Cat and Binah Puss, for being so distracting.

Thank you Moxie Nox for her wonderful squirrel photograph, the only card for which I wasn't able to take a picture myself that I was happy with. You can see more of her wonderful photography here: www.moxienox.com.

I wish to send out huge thanks to the online community of Tarot enthusiasts, fellow artists, writers, and friends whose support and feedback has been invaluable as ever!

Finally I must thank you, reading this now, for your support. May you never want for sticks, din-dins, or doggy love!

CONTENTS

Foreword *by Barbara Moore ---8*
Introduction *by Emily Carding ---10*

The Cards---*12*

Now 14
Innocence 16
Vision 18
Crossing 20
Freedom 22
Waiting 24
Journey 26
Walkies 28
Splash 30
Deep thoughts 32
Alpha 34

GUARDIAN 36	
REST 38	
FRIENDS 40	LOVE 72
FAMILY 42	MAGIC 74
DIN-DINS 44	FETCH 76
DOG JAIL 46	NEMESIS 78
SORRY 48	RESIGNATION 80
SHARING 50	BRAVE 82
BARK 52	RUNNING 84
THE WILD 54	ROLL OVER 86
SAD 56	SQUIRREL! 88
SCENT 58	BIG STICK 90
TRACKS 60	PLAYTIME 92
LEAP 62	LOYALTY 94
BEG 64	WOLF 96
TREAT 66	ADVENTURE 98
VET 68	GOOD BOY 100
HAPPY 70	

How to Use the Cards ---*102*
Conclusion ---*110*
About the Authors ---*110*

FOREWORD
~Barbara Moore

We met during an unforgettable week in the summer of 2010. During that week of wonders, we spent stolen moments cuddling and playing joyful games of fetch. Every morning, we woke up early, before anyone else in the house, so that we could wander across the moors of Cornwall, just the two of us. While it was only five short days, I went home transformed.

All dogs have so much to offer. But Albus Dumbledog is a dog among dogs! Although you may not have the opportunity to visit Albus, you can now, through these cards, revel in his wisdom. He shares his musings on a wide range of subjects. Throughout his daily life, Albus does experience a good many things, as do we all. The thing with humans, though, is often we are not present enough to see and feel and really experience each moment of our lives.

During our morning walkies, Albus led me through gates, over bridges, along rivers, and across fields. Because I didn't know the area, I was often anxious, worried that I wouldn't find my way back. The wilds of Cornwall are very different from the streets of St. Paul, Minnesota, my hometown. But Albus was determined and helped me learn about Crossing (page 20).

Albus was already familiar with the areas we walked and so he could show me treasures. The land (see The Wild, page 54) is woven with Magic (page 74). While I was quite expecting to feel the magic in spectacular trees or unique stones, sometimes Albus reminded me that magic, and sometimes even fairies, can be found in very common-looking items, if only we take the time to see them.

For five days, I luxuriated in my new Friend (page 40x), enjoying the simple Love (page 72) he offered. And then I learned a new lesson. Resignation (page 80). It was time to say goodbye and go home. My own darling dogs, Whiskey and Norman, waited there for me to return, and I would be happy to see them. But Albus, well; Albus is something special, as you will soon discover for yourself!

Before I say good-bye here, let me thank Albus's owner, photographer, and ghost writer, Emily Carding. If she had not invited an almost complete stranger to spend a week in her home, a magical converted chapel, my life would indeed be much poorer. Emily, and Albus, I thank you both from the bottom of my heart, which you made fuller, wiser, and happier.

BARBARA MOORE
St. Paul, Minnesota
November 2011

Barbara Moore is an internationally beloved Tarot author, reader, and teacher who has written numerous books on the subject, including a large number of companion books for popular decks. To learn more about Barbara's work, please visit:

http: www.practicaltarotreadings.com

Introduction
~Emily Carding

Simple Wisdom of the Household Dog started as a joke. Just one of those crazy ideas you have when sitting around the dinner table chatting that, somehow, went on to gain a life and momentum all of its own, as well as a surprising amount of substance. I had already at this point created a number of Tarot and Oracle decks, which although rendered in intuitively accessible ways, deal with complex ideas and esoteric systems. "Wouldn't it be great if Albus created an oracle deck?" I found myself saying to my husband one evening. "It could have cards like 'stick' and 'walkies'... Wouldn't that be fun?" After some time laughing about the idea and throwing around a few card titles between us, I looked through already existing photographs of Albus and picked a few that had a clear story or emotion behind them, chose a card title, and posted them online. These first few cards had an immediate and positive response from people and I realised that it *was* a fun idea, but it was more than that. It was a fun idea that hadn't been done before and that could actually really work as a quirky and perceptive oracle.

You see, people don't often talk about or consider the wisdom of dogs, nor extol their spiritual or mystical qualities. Cats definitely have one over on them there. And dolphins, of course. Hence the very large number of oracle and tarot decks you may find featuring cats or dolphins, (possibly not both together yet, but it's only a matter of time.) What we *do* note about our canine companions is their love of life, their loyalty, their innate trustworthiness and honesty- their *simple* natures. Love of life? Loyalty? Honesty? All sounds like wisdom to me. *Simple* wisdom.

Wisdom does not need to be searched for solely in ancient texts or new age concepts of lightworking and ascension. Indeed, in order for it to have any impact on our lives, to really mean anything to the person who has to do the washing up and pay the bills every day, it is vital that it is found in the very simplest things. Dogs are very good at this. In fact, they truly are the masters of simple wisdom, with their innate ability to completely exist in the moment, a state of mind sought by many and achieved by few in our hectic modern lifestyles.

As my good friend and accomplished tarot and oracles author Barbara Moore pointed out in her generous Foreword, Albus is not just any dog. Everyone who meets him falls in love with him, and it is his extraordinarily expressive face and ability to convey a story and atmosphere that really makes this deck work. This oracle is a photographic journey into the daily life of a household dog, and within the experiences that Albus so kindly shares with us we can all find lessons and guidance for our own lives. With Albus as your guide, may you all find your own road to simple wisdom…

Albus Says…

Actually, the whole thing was my idea, but these human creative types get so confused when ideas come into their heads, they rarely really know where they've come from. I've seen a few of these Tarot and oracle decks floating about the place, and I have to say they don't make much sense to me. Except I noticed that some of the Tarot decks have a lot of sticks in. I like that. I don't understand why that chap carrying ten sticks looks so woebegone though, I would be delighted! Ten sticks! Cool!

Anyway, I looked at all these things and realised that I may not be an ascended-indigo-dolphin-archangel-from-Atlantis, but I do know a thing or two about what's important in life. I would like to share that with you! Thankfully, my owner seems to enjoy taking photos, and let's be honest, I do enjoy posing, so bringing you this little window into my world has been enjoyable for both of us. I hope that using it will be enjoyable for you, too!

The Cards

Beg

The Wild

Good Boy

Journey

The following pages contain brief accounts of the significance of every card in the deck. They should be useful for you to refer to as you start to use the cards, but don't be afraid to come up with your own meanings, too! All of us have our own particular set of personal symbols that grow within us as we live our lives, and this is your most profound resource. As you look through the cards, you may wish to make notes of your first instinctive responses to the images or any thoughts you may have about them. Do they remind you of any particular time in your life? Do they evoke a feeling, a memory, or even a smell? Keeping a record of all these impressions will significantly help to make using the cards a rewarding experience for you.

There are many possible uses for oracle cards. The most obvious and well known is, of course, divination, but they can also be used for storytelling and meditation. You may want to consider using this particular set of cards for translating communications from your pet! Once we have looked at the individual cards, the last section of the book gives you some ideas of how to use them for yourself and others — enjoy!

Now

EXIST ∞ BE ∞ AWARE ∞ SIMPLICITY ∞ THE PRESENT

Albus says…

Dogs can't keep secrets. We don't have them! So I'm giving it all away right at the beginning – the key to the simple wisdom of the household dog. It's Now. I don't lose myself in what might be or what has been, or might going to *maybe* be, like you do! I am here, now, fully in the moment. It's great! Join me. Don't let the moment pass you by, however simple it is. Pause. Paws! There is beauty in the moment. Beauty in breath, in life… Sometimes it's obvious, like the rainbow, sometimes less obvious, like the texture of mud, but it's there!

Now

Owner's Notes:

Well, Albus summed that up very nicely. This really is one of the wonderful things about dogs, their ability to exist completely in the moment.

If you have drawn this card, it is telling you to stop worrying about the past or the future and simply be in the moment. Easier said than done for us humans, true. Look around you. Stop for a moment and breathe and be grateful for that breath. If you can ground yourself in the moment and find some beauty in it, something to be grateful for, then you will find a strength in that ability that will serve you well in life. Every moment is a gift. What gift is Now offering *you*?

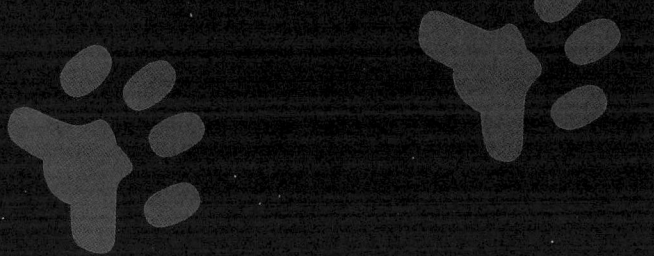

INNOCENCE

WONDER ∞ FRESHNESS ∞ EXPLORATION ∞ DISCOVERY ∞ CHILD-LIKE

Albus says…

Was that me? I don't remember being that small…though I do keep hearing about how I ate a certain person's trainers. They must have been yummy. Apparently I also ate the kitchen furniture. But I didn't know any better then, I'm a good boy now. Look how cute I was! I'm cute now too of course—some things don't change. Perhaps in a more rugged way… What was I saying? Oh yes, I don't remember being that small… I suppose we were all that small once?

Owner's Notes

Yes, those were *my* trainers, and indeed he did eat the kitchen furniture. It was all part of his journey of discovery, his way of exploring the world when everything was new. We've all done things we shouldn't have, but we learn from those mistakes and hopefully don't make the same errors too many times! Albus doesn't eat shoes or furniture now, but he still looks at the world with the same puppy eyes, full of wonder.

We should never let go completely of our INNOCENCE. True, we learn and we grow, but we can continue to learn and grow in our understanding so much more if we can keep the wonder-filled eyes of a child.

Innocence

VISION

PROSPECTS ∞ POTENTIAL ∞ UNVEILING ∞ CLARITY ∞ TRUTH

Albus says...

Wow! I can see for miles! Look at that world out there, full of sticks and mud and endless possibilities. Everything is so clear! There is nothing to stop me, nothing in my way. I could just run and run... Or I could stop and watch the world unfold before me. What a wonderful world it is!

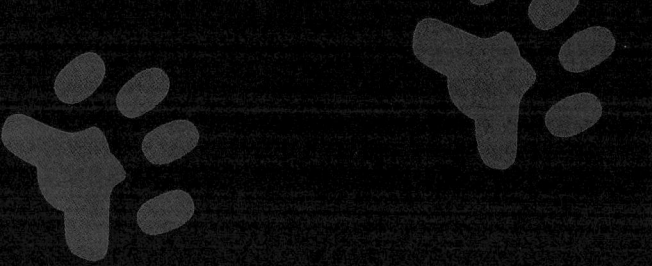

Owner's Notes

Albus is right; it is a wonderful world, and great possibilities are now revealing themselves to you.

This card shows one of those moments when everything becomes so clear, you wonder why you couldn't see it before. It is as though you not only see a path laid out before you, but *every* path and every possibility, and realise your innate power to choose. You are being offered a Vision of the bigger picture and your part in it. The world reveals itself to you in all its glory and the only limit is your imagination.

Vision

CROSSING

TRANSITION ∞ MOVEMENT ∞ CHANGE ∞ FLEXIBILITY ∞ EVOLUTION

Albus says...

Oh, I love crossing the bridge! One side of it is near home, after going *down* the hill, and then the other side goes off into the woods and *up* the hill, and then to the wide-open moorland! It's quite different on one side to the other side. I like both sides, and I like the sound my paws make as I run across. I like to splash in the water underneath as well, but don't like to swim all the way across. Sometimes the water is rough or too deep for me. But with the bridge, I can get to the other side with no problem!

Crossing

Owner's Notes

Crossing a bridge is the easiest thing in the world, yet some of us might be afraid of what lies on the other side, or underneath, or whether the bridge will hold us up. Albus teaches us that not only is there nothing to be afraid of, there's plenty to enjoy. Even the process of crossing from one place, or one way of being, to another can be fun!

This card speaks about a change of location or circumstances and a smooth transition from one to the other. Links with the past are not lost, the door remains open, but a new land beckons. Welcome it with open arms and you will not regret it.

FREEDOM

LIBERATION ∞ OPTIMISM ∞ OPENNESS ∞ EXPANSION ∞ CHOICE

Albus says…

When I was but a young pup and first saw the sea, it was so big and different from anything I had ever seen that I just barked and barked! When we're not used to it, being without boundaries can be strange and even scary. Now it's one of my favourite places. So much space! So much freedom! I can dig if I want to, splash if I want to, and sniff the bottoms of other dogs to my heart's content. There's no path to follow here; just write your own rules and forge your own self. Go ahead. Sniff that horizon. Or that bottom if you prefer. I know I do.

Owner's Notes

Freedom to do as we like is a rare gift, one that gets taken for granted so often by those who have it, and so heartily sought by those who don't. As human beings, we are constrained by ideas of society and "proper" behaviour and, on a more sinister level, our lives and wishes are often taken out of our control by supposedly "higher" powers – not those of a spiritual nature, but governments and financially motivated organisations.

We should all learn from Albus and enjoy the opportunity to feel free when it arises, and appreciate the freedoms that we are lucky enough to possess. Do not agonise over decisions, but rather relish the fact that you have the power to make them. Above all, always reach for the horizon, and never take the feeling of the wind in your hair for granted…

Freedom

Waiting

Anticipation ∞ Patience ∞ Precognition ∞ Intuition ∞ Connection

Albus says...

Where did you go? I miss you when you're gone, you know. Never mind, I'm sure you'll be back soon... In fact, I always know when you'll be back and I do so like to give you a warm welcome! I'll just sit here for a while and chat with Anubis... Any minute now. Any...minute...now?

Owner's Notes

All dog owners have noticed that their dogs always seem to know when they'll be back, even if there isn't a regular routine. It's one of their special charms, and they are always ready to greet you as though they haven't seen you for years!

This card speaks of those times of anticipation, when nothing is tangibly happening, but you have a sense that it is just about to. Be patient, it won't be long! Any minute now, in fact…

Waiting

Journey

Travel ∞ Destination ∞ Trust ∞ Transport ∞ Fate

Albus says…

Oh, I'm excited; we're going in the car! That means we're going somewhere. I don't know where, though… I hope it's somewhere nice. I'm sure you'd let me drive if I could, but my paws can't grip the wheel very well and I can't reach the pedals at the same time…and when I *can* reach the pedals, I can't see where I'm going. Apparently, that doesn't end well. So I'll just sit here and enjoy the ride! We could be going to the beach, to the town…or the vet's. Gosh. Who knows? Well, I'll find out soon enough. I trust you!

Owner's Notes

Sometimes we have to put our destinies in the hands of others. Actually, we do this on a daily basis without even thinking about it! On a mundane level, if we catch a bus, train, plane, or taxi, or even when we drive ourselves, we trust that others will not do something foolish or unsafe and that we will reach our destination.

This card could easily speak about this kind of journey, but Albus also teaches us more about the spiritual level of this trust. We are all being taken somewhere in our lives, and there are times when it seems as though it is out of our hands. Synchronistic events and meetings give us signs that something or someone is guiding us in a particular direction. When this happens, it is best to trust and enjoy the journey.

Journey

Walkies

Exercise ∞ Routine ∞ Hobbies ∞ Fitness ∞ Guidance

Albus says...

My favourite part of the day! I love getting out and about. For some parts, I need to stay on my lead so that I don't get carried away and chase things I shouldn't...like sheep and cows... and cars... But a lot of the time I get let off the lead and have a good old romp about. I try not to go too far though. I wouldn't want to get separated from my owner, of course, in case they get lost. Exercise is so important! I want to stay bouncy and fit for as long as I can, and my owners too, so I make sure we go out every day.

Owner's Notes

I must admit it's my favourite part of the day too, and it certainly feels as though I'm the one being taken for the walk most of the time, as is often pointed out to me by passers by, much to their amusement. We all have our routines and structure to our daily lives, some more than others, but generally we all have part of the day we look forward to. The great thing about Walkies is that not only is it enjoyable and gets us out in the open air, but it also keeps us fit, especially with all the hills around here.

This card could be advising you to find something enjoyable to work into your daily or weekly routine that helps to keep you active and happy. It could also suggest that you can do so best under someone else's guidance or "lead." (Haha.)

Walkies

SPLASH

DECISIVENESS ∞ SPONTANEITY ∞ VIVACIOUSNESS ∞ IMPACT ∞ EFFECT

Albus says...

Don't hang around watching from the sidelines; get in there! Make a big splash! That's what I like to do. No messing about, just "weeeee, splash!" I do think people are funny when they put their toes in, out, and in again. The water's lovely, so get on with it! Don't waste time on indecision; you'll love it when you get in. You're going to get wet anyway if you're standing around when I jump in. *Everyone* knows about it when I arrive! I may spend some time drying off afterwards, but boy is it worth it!

Owner's Notes

If there's something you're thinking about doing, but you're feeling uncertain, why not just take Albus's advice and dive in? You can make a big impact, and send ripples of positive effects out into the world when you act decisively.

Whatever it is that is causing you to be hesitant will soon melt away if you simply go for it! You may well inspire others to follow your lead. The water *does* look lovely…

Splash

DEEP THOUGHTS

REVERIE ∞ REFLECTION ∞ PHILOSOPHY ∞ DAYDREAMS ∞ INACTION

Albus says...

I KNOW THAT PEOPLE SOMETIMES GET LOST IN deep thoughts about things like, "Why is the sky blue?" "What is the nature of freedom?" and "Where do all the teaspoons go?" I understand. Sometimes we dogs have deep thoughts too, like, "What's that smell?" "Is it dinner time?" and "When will she stop taking pictures of me and take me for a walk?"

Owner's Notes

Poor Albus! Soon, I promise.

This card may indicate that you are in a state of thoughtfulness and reverie, perhaps reminiscing about the past, dreaming about the future, or pondering a present conundrum. Whatever the case, you are inclined more towards inner reflection than action at the moment, but be careful not to neglect those around you while you lose yourself in your world of thoughts.

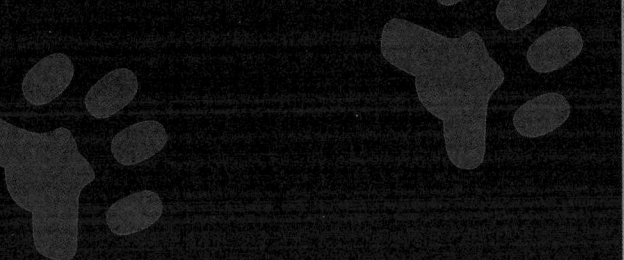

Deep Thoughts

Alpha

Success ∞ Career ∞ Leadership ∞ Promotion ∞ Fame

Albus says…

Look at me! I made it to the top. Behold, I am mighty! Climbing to the top of things can be tiring, but it sure is a great feeling when you reach the top. I feel so proud of myself, like the alpha dog of the world! Everything else seems so small, and the sky is so close and so big. Well, this is as high up as I can get, I think I'll stay up here for a little while. Not forever though; no, that would be too long. I would be sure to get lonely after a while…

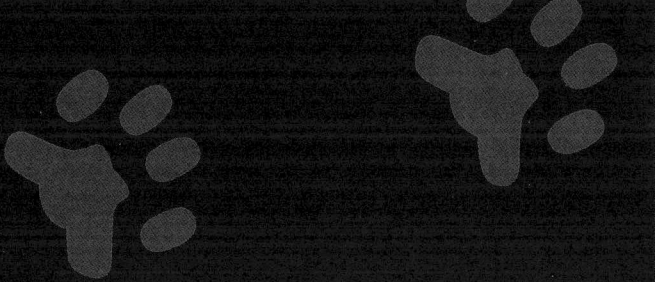

Owner's Notes

Now don't let it go to your head, Albus! It's not likely. Dogs don't tend to suffer from issues of over-inflated egos.

This card may indicate either a personal breakthrough or career success, with something that you have worked hard on finally paying off. This could put you in a position of leadership and responsibility. Achievement after continued effort is certainly worth celebrating, so enjoy the feeling! As Albus rightly points out though, it can be lonely at the top of the world, so be sure not to isolate yourself with feelings of superiority.

Alpha

Guardian

Defence ∞ Protection ∞ Wariness ∞ Preparation ∞ Caution

Albus says...

It's not all fun and frolics you know, being a dog. We take our responsibilities very seriously! Underneath this soft and lovable exterior is an alert and poised warrior, ready for action. True, most of the time anyone comes along I just try to hug them and see if they have any treats, but that's because most of the people I meet smell friendly. Every so often though, someone I meet smells "off" and I make sure they don't come near my people! I am always ready for action. Grrrrrr!

Owner's Notes

Albus's pose in this photo is reminiscent of many statues of the Ancient Egyptian God, Anubis, who guards the gates to the Underworld. Even if your dog is a beloved (and soppy) member of the family and not a trained guard dog, you can bet he'll still have a good nose for danger.

Now is a time for caution and alertness, keeping those who are important to you safe. There's no need to be paranoid, but simply keep your wits about you in your dealings with others and listen to your instincts.

Guardian

Rest

Break ∞ Relax ∞ Pause ∞ Breathe ∞ Meditation

Albus says...

Phew! Time for a breather. I love to run around but I do get tired after a bit, and it's nice to stop and enjoy the scenery. If you never stop to breathe and look around, well you could end up anywhere at all—and exhausted to boot! So I'm just going to lie here for a while and enjoy the squishy moss and the sunbeam, thank you very much. Why not pull up a rock and join me?

Owner's Notes

We can't run on full thrusters every minute of the day without exhausting ourselves or making ourselves ill. We can stop it from getting to that level by making sure that we take a break. We can look back at where we've come from, plan where we're going next, and take a good few deep breaths before the next adventure.

As Albus rightly points out, if we don't take the time to restore ourselves and clear our heads we could find ourselves somewhere we never planned to be, wondering how we got there.

Rest

FRIENDS

SOCIALISING ∞ FUN ∞ COMPANY ∞ CONVERSATION ∞ SHARED INTERESTS

Albus says…

ONCE WE'VE SNIFFED EACH OTHER'S BOTTOMS A few times, we're sure to become good friends! We can all be different sizes and breeds and it doesn't matter at all; we get along so well and have a wonderful time. It's fun to run around together, roll around together, and then run around some more. Running around on your own can be good, too, but it's so much more fun with friends! What do you like to do with your friends? You humans are so funny with your social complexities. If you are sometimes shy and don't have many friends, try sniffing a few bottoms and I'm sure that you'll soon have lots.

Owner's Notes

Albus has his own special doggy way of making friends, but it's rarely this simple for humans. Our ways seem so strange to him! Because our friendships are forged in such complex ways, we should treasure them all the more.

This card suggests it's time to enjoy an activity you can share with others, or simply spend some time in good company. You never know when you're going to make new friends; it can happen in the most unexpected ways…though with all respect to Albus's wisdom, I'd pass on the bottom sniffing for now.

Friends

FAMILY

HOME ∞ RELATIONS ∞ CONNECTION ∞ SAFETY ∞ APPRECIATION

Albus says...

I'M SO HAPPY WHEN ALL THE MEMBERS OF THE pack are together, like we are meant to be. There always seems to be something-or-other keeping somebody-or-other away, but it means we enjoy the time we have together even more. Members of a pack should never take each other for granted; we all have important roles to play and our own responsibilities to each other. Always appreciate each other and never let anyone in your pack feel neglected, because everyone should feel loved at home. My role is simple. I am the dog. If you ask me, I have a pretty good deal!

Owner's Notes

Those we share our home with, be they furry or not, can be the easiest to take for granted, yet truly they are precious to us.

We should never be too busy to show those who are closest to us how much they mean to us. As Albus knows, simple is best, so simply by spending time together you can show your family just how special and valued they are.

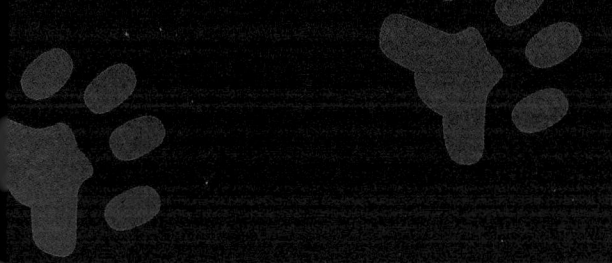

Family

DIN-DINS

NUTRITION ∞ DIET ∞ COMFORT ∞ BALANCE ∞ NURTURE

Albus says...

I LOVE TO EAT! I'LL EAT WHATEVER I CAN GET HOLD of, but I know that whatever my owners give me will be good for me. I wouldn't have any energy to run and play without a good din-dins every day, so I make sure to eat it all up as quickly as I can. Plus it's always yummy! Om nom nom nom! Maybe if I eat extra quickly, they'll forget that they've fed me and give me some more... especially if I make my eyes really big and do my best to look really hungry... Is it working?

Owner's Notes

No Albus, it is *not* working, but nice try. If we just keep feeding you, you'll turn into a big lump of a dog and you won't be able to run and play then, either!

Balance of nutrition is so important for health, and we should all make sure that we keep ourselves healthy by maintaining a good diet. Albus is always so grateful for his din-dins, and we can follow his example by always being grateful for a good meal.

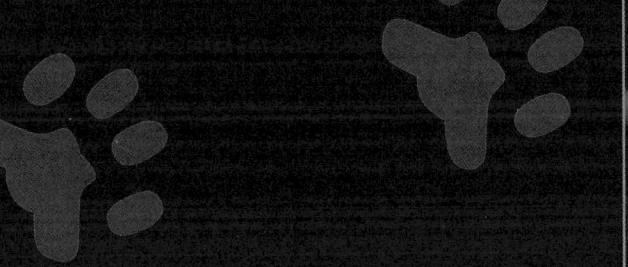

Dog Jail

RESTRICTION ∞ BOUNDARIES ∞ DISCIPLINE ∞ PUNISHMENT ∞ FRUSTRATION

Albus says…

But I'm innocent! I wasn't even there, wherever there is or whatever happened! I am imprisoned for a crime I did not commit! Why are you doing this to meeeeee? I feel like I've been in here forever. I want to feel the wind in my fur and the rain on my nose again. I have forgotten what the sky looks like! Let me out! Please? I'll be good, I promise!

Owner's Notes

Oh Albus, you can be such a drama queen sometimes! You've only been in there five minutes; you just need to stay there so I can get this mess cleaned up without you under my feet. Now you just hush up like a good boy and I'm sure you'll be able to come out very soon…

Like Albus, we don't always think about or see the bigger picture when we feel that we're being constricted or held back, but often it is for our own good. It can be frustrating, but when the time is right you'll be able to move forward again.

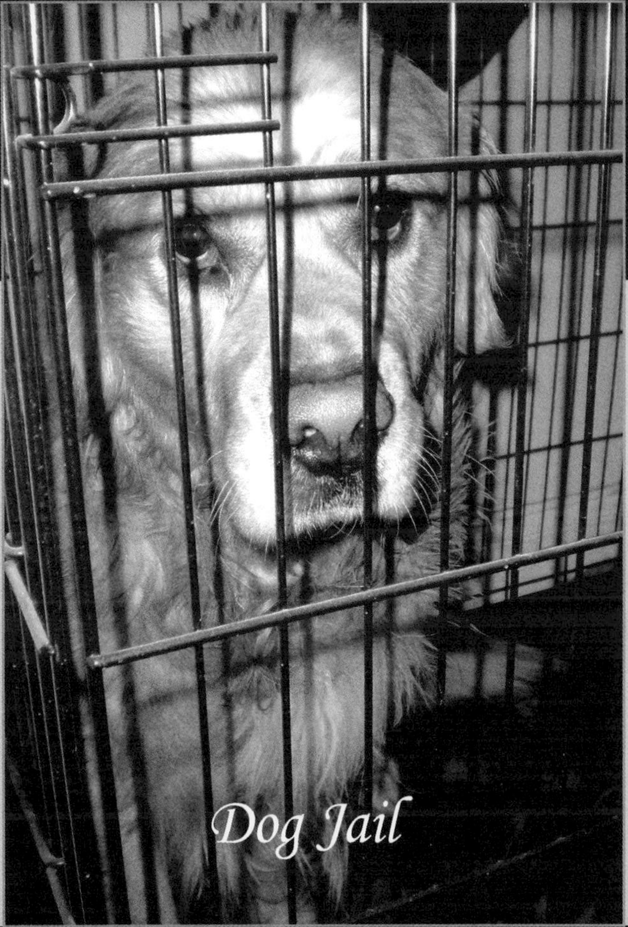

Dog Jail

Sorry

Responsibility ∞ Guilt ∞ Confession ∞ Blame ∞ Forgiveness

Albus says...

I confess. This time it really was me. I didn't mean to, though; it's just that sometimes I can't help myself and the next thing I know… well, it's too late. I truly am sorry! I really will try so very hard not to do it again. Please forgive me? We dogs really have no concept of lying or trying to cover things up like you strange folk sometimes do. Haven't you realised that it just makes everything harder, stressful and complicated?

Owner's Notes

It's hard to stay cross with Albus with those big brown eyes! It's an expression that might be worth trying to cultivate if, like Albus, you've got something to apologise for.

This card might suggest that it's time to swallow your pride and accept responsibility for your actions, even if they were accidental, and make amends. The blame may be harsh at first, but openness and honesty are much more likely to lead to peace than avoidance and deception.

Sorry

Sharing

Empathy ∞ Openness ∞ Kindness ∞ Generosity ∞ Compassion

Albus says…

*I*f you're ever feeling a bit lonely, you come out with me and tell me your troubles. I'll listen! You'll be smiling again before long. I know that human life can sometimes seem overwhelming, but there's no need to keep it all inside, you know. Why don't you share your problems with me, and I'll share my wisdom with you. I will also share cuddles—that always seems to work a treat!

Owner's Notes

As Albus has already pointed out a number of times, our lives do tend to be much more complicated than his. We can sometimes carry our problems and responsibilities like a heavy burden, not realising that we don't have to shoulder it all alone.

We all need a kind ear sometimes, and though a furry ear may not always understand exactly what it is that is bothering us, sometimes simply sharing is enough to lighten the load.

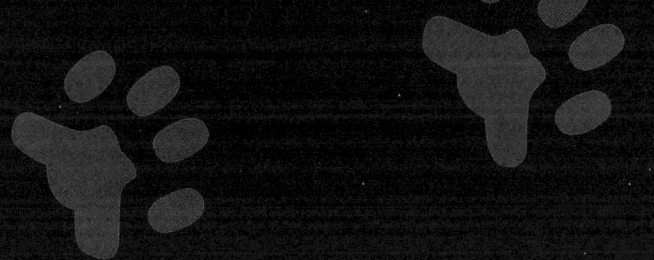

Sharing

Bark

Warning ∞ Expression ∞ Communication ∞ Alarm ∞ Surprise

Albus says…

WOOF, WOOF, WOOF! I BARK WHEN I'M EXCITED or scared or if something seems a bit weird. Sometimes I bark when I get impatient, too! My point is, that if I *didn't* bark, then you wouldn't *know* and it might just be important. Little Timmy might be stuck down the well or something like that. That's what that dog on the telly was barking about.

Owner's Notes

Albus generally doesn't bark a lot, so we pay attention when he does. If there's something happening at the moment that you're unsure about, be sure to make your concern known. Even if it turns out to be nothing, it's better to be safe than sorry!

Equally, this card may indicate that someone is trying to tell you something important, or the card itself may be warning you that something surprising may be about to happen or to pay more attention to things around you.

Bark

THE WILD

NATURE ∞ WILDERNESS ∞ PRIMAL ∞ UNLEASHED ∞ ANCESTORS

Albus says…

THERE'S POWER IN THE LAND, CAN YOU FEEL IT? I can. A power that makes my fur stand on end, makes my paws run fast across the earth, and lights my eyes with green fire! We all need to feel this sometimes, running through the trees like those who have gone before must have done so many times. Now they are bones beneath our feet…mmmm…bones… Where was I? Oh, yes. Feel the power of the land and let go of modern life for a while; you'll feel better for it!

Owner's Notes

Albus is right; there is strength and deep healing to be found in the green places of the world and that could be what's needed for you right now.

Let your hair down and feel the rhythm of the natural world. Spend time out in the wild and forget about the demands that wait in the "civilised" world. We all need time to recharge our batteries, immersing ourselves in the primal power of the land. Can you hear the call of the wild?

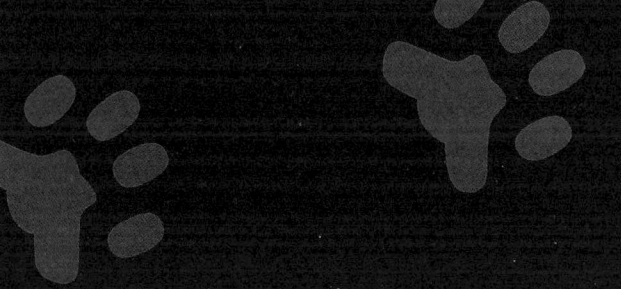

The Wild

SAD

NEGLECT ∞ MOODS ∞ LONELINESS ∞ WALLOWING ∞ DEPRESSION

Albus says…

We all have down moods sometimes, even us dogs. When we feel sad, we don't try to hide it or put a brave face on it; we just let ourselves feel sad until something happens to cheer us up, like maybe a hug, or a stick, or walkies, or until we just feel happier. Mostly, I am sad when I am left on my own, but its never for too long. Something might have happened to make us feel sad, or we could just be feeling sad for no real reason, but whatever it is, it's sure to pass soon enough. It's all part of life!

Owner's Notes

We do have a tendency to try to cover up our feelings if we're feeling down, sad, or lonely, but that can lead to deeper problems if we don't deal with the cause or simply acknowledge that there is something wrong.

Often the acknowledgement of difficult emotions can be the first stage in coming through them, so if you are feeling sad, allow yourself to feel it and do not feel ashamed. None of us are happy all of the time, not even Albus! As Albus himself says, "It will pass."

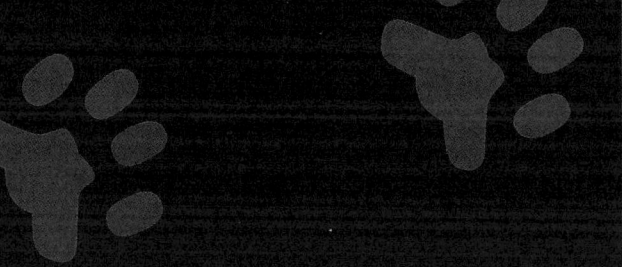

Sad

Scent

Senses ∞ Detection ∞ Messages ∞ Identity ∞ Discovery

Albus says...

Scent is so important to us dogs! We really don't understand how you all manage with your underdeveloped nostrils. Scent creates a whole vivid landscape of colour for our senses; it is the texture and meaning behind everything we see and hear. I know what and who's been where, and why and when! I can leave messages for others, too, so that they know who I am and where I go. Smells are so much better than words—they show us so much, and never lie.

Owner's Notes

I'm amazed Albus didn't mention his love of bottom sniffing again here. It's true, dogs have a remarkable sense of smell that gives them reams of information about the world around them. Although our sense of smell is nowhere near as keen as Albus's, our senses are taking in information all the time and building a highly detailed picture of the world in our subconscious.

There may be important messages for you if you pay attention to the signs around you. Open your senses and be aware; you may uncover interesting clues!

Scent

Tracks

Memory ∞ Record ∞ Legacy ∞ Impact ∞ Effect

Albus says…

Wherever I go, I leave tracks — so do you! Not always as obvious as these ones here in the snow, but they're there alright. It's nothing to worry about, so long as you don't go to places that you shouldn't! We can follow other dog's and people's tracks, too, if we want to. Together, we make a pattern of tracks all across the world…

Owner's Notes

Albus doesn't worry too much about leaving tracks, but as humans, we maybe have a little more to consider. Everything we do and everywhere we go, we leave traces and there are consequences.

From the "carbon footprint" we all create through our travel and daily lives to the trace we leave of our activities on the internet, we are all making tracks every day of our lives. When we are mindful of the effects our actions have, we can consciously create a positive impact on the world.

Tracks

LEAP

CONFIDENCE ∞ PROGRESS ∞ OBSTACLES ∞ BELIEF ∞ MOMENTUM

Albus says…

I CAN FLY! NOTHING CAN GET IN MY WAY! It doesn't matter how rocky the terrain or what obstacles there might be, I just leap right over them. It's a wonderful feeling, like being unstoppable, and all you have to do is believe in yourself! If I slowed down or faltered every time I came across a fallen tree or a boulder, I wouldn't get very far at all. Best thing to do is leap with confidence!

Owner's Notes

Our leaps may take a number of different forms. We can take leaps in understanding, leaps of faith, or literal leaps if we like extreme sports!

In any case, this card refers to the ability to surmount any obstacle with ease. A certain momentum of success has been achieved which cannot be slowed down by any minor considerations. Do not allow negativity from others or unfortunate occurrences to get in the way of your plans. Simply leap with confidence and continue on your path, just as Albus shows us!

Leap

BEG

Manipulation ∞ Desire ∞ Shameless ∞ Greed ∞ Need

Albus says…

Pleasepleasepleasepleaseplease! Oh, that smells so nice. Please can I have some? I'll be good! Look how good I am. I'm so good and I love you so much. If you loved me, you'd give me some, and I know you do, so I'm sure you will. I have no pride. I'll beg as much as it takes. I'll sit. I'll lie down. I'll make my eyes really big. Pleeeeeeeeease?

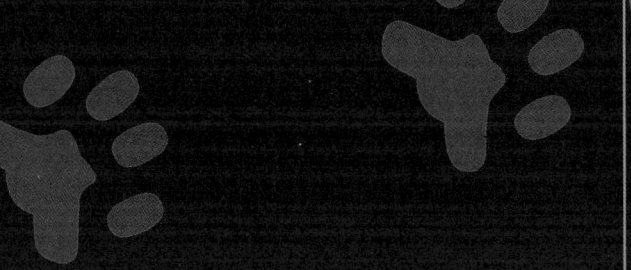

Owner's Notes

All dog owners will no doubt be aware of their canine companion's uncanny ability to detect food of any kind the second it appears, and the lengths he or she will go to in order to acquire some.

When this card appears, we might ask ourselves whether we are being similarly undignified in our pursuit of our desires, and whether or not it's worth it. Of course, if you decide it *is* worth it, then by all means, take some lessons from Albus here. The big puppy eyes technique does seem to work very well with most people!

Beg

Treat

PRAISE ∞ PAMPERING ∞ INDULGENCE ∞ ACKNOWLEDGEMENT ∞ AWARD

Albus says...

Oh, what a nice surprise! Treats are the tastiest tit-bits you could ever taste. They can be anything from tiny little biscuits to a whole yummy sausage, and they always make me happy. Treats let me know that I've been a good boy, and I always try to be the best boy I can be. The best thing about treats is that I know they're always given with love. That's the tastiest bit!

Owner's Notes

We all need a treat every now and then! Like Albus, we might be lucky enough to receive ours for good behaviour, perhaps for excelling at what we do, or perhaps simply from someone who wants to give a sign of their affection. As humans, we are in the privileged position of being able to treat ourselves if no one else is forthcoming.

Whatever the case may be, when this card appears, you are due a treat. Go ahead and enjoy – you've earned it!

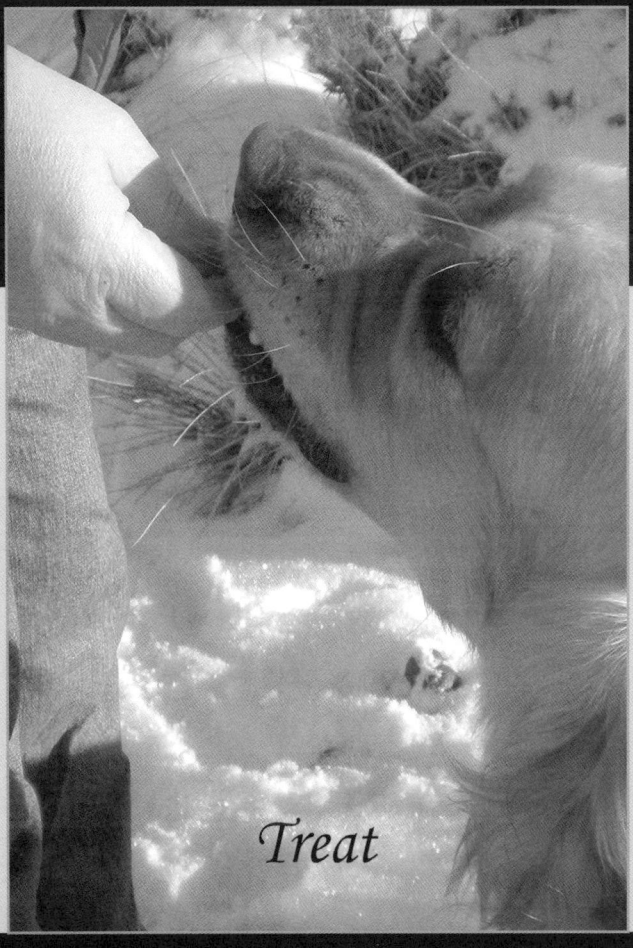

Treat

Vet

Health ∞ Medicine ∞ Healing ∞ Care ∞ Trust

Albus says...

A LOT OF MY FELLOW FURRY FRIENDS ARE NOT fans of the vet at *all* and hide from their owners on days when they are due to visit. I actually don't mind it all that much. I get lots of attention, there are always interesting smells, and I get to meet new dogs and people. I know that it's for my own good and that the vet just needs to check that I'm healthy—and keep me that way. I am pleased to say that I keep myself in fine shape, so there's nothing to worry about!

Owner's Notes

Albus knows how important it is to keep healthy and that the vet is only there to help him.

All of us should pay attention to our health, as without that, what do we have? Sometimes, it may be that we have to pay a visit to a medical practitioner for an examination, diagnosis, or treatment. Often we can be reluctant to do so, as we don't want to hear bad news or indeed be poked around with, but we need to be able to trust that they are there to help us and that we will receive the care we need from a qualified expert.

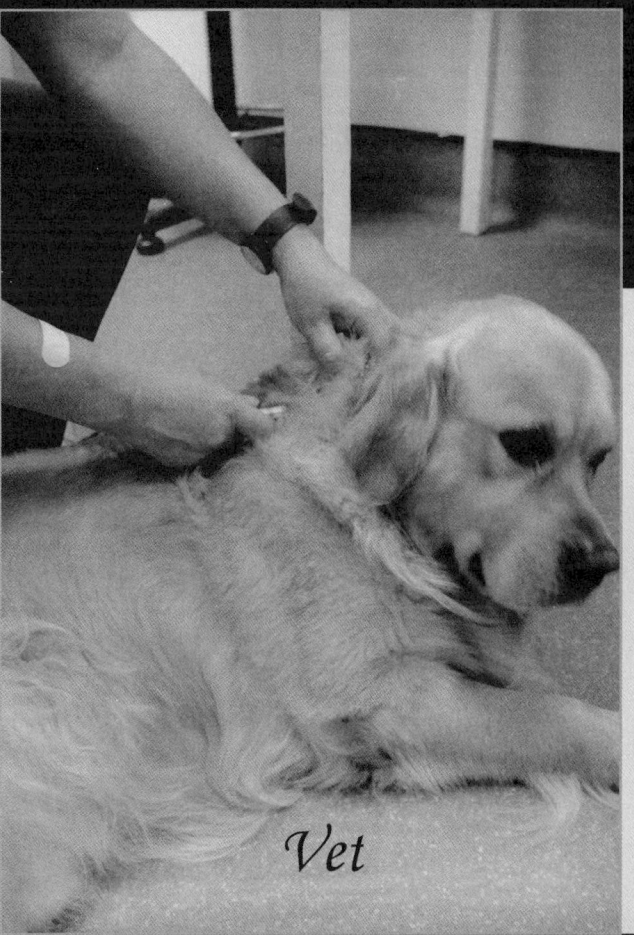

Vet

Happy

Gratitude ∞ Celebration ∞ Joy ∞ Fulfilment ∞ Bliss

Albus says…

There's always something to be happy about! I am happy most of the time, but sometimes I am really, *really* happy, especially if I've had a particularly good walk or a nice din-dins. People and other dogs to play with make me happy, too. Cuddles always make me happy. (Surely they make everybody happy?) Sticks make me happy. (That's definitely a dog thing, apparently.) Having a warm, safe home and people who care for me makes me happy everyday. Sunshine makes me happy, but then so does rain, because then I can splash in puddles! It's all a matter of how we choose to see the world, I suppose…

Owner's Notes

Dogs can usually find something to be happy about, but it's not so easy for us humans sometimes. This may be because we tend to dwell on matters, whereas dogs have the enviable ability to exist completely in the present moment. There is much to be learned from this simplicity, as with it comes an appreciation of all the things around us that we should be grateful for, but too often take for granted.

What is your equivalent of a good stick to chew? Every ray of sunlight and breath we take is indeed a blessing that can bring us great happiness when we can allow ourselves to let go of unnecessary hindrances. Just as we can find ourselves feeling sad for no apparent reason, so too can we find ourselves in an unaccountably good mood. On these days, embrace every moment of happiness: It is a gift truly to be grateful for.

Happy

LOVE

DEVOTION ∞ OPENNESS ∞ TRUST ∞ CARE ∞ COMMITMENT

Albus says...

*L*OVE IS THE MOST IMPORTANT THING THERE IS. It might be more important than din-dins or even sniffing bottoms, but truthfully it's a part of everything we are and do in life. You humans seem to make it a very complicated matter, introducing all kinds of baffling conditions and rules, but for me, love is life. I love life and I live love and I love you – even if we haven't met! I'm sure we'd get on wonderfully if we did meet. Can you open your heart to love? It's simple! Give love generously to the world without expectation or conditions, and you will feel the love within the earth itself and everything within, around, and above it! The best place to start is with yourself.

Love

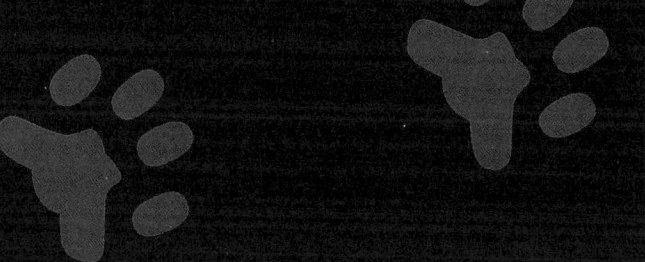

Owner's Notes

Dogs do have an extraordinary capacity for unconditional love, a trait that is sadly sometimes abused by those who do not appreciate it.

We can learn from Albus's great and generous heart but should not make the mistake of allowing ourselves to be betrayed or mistreated. Love does not only mean love for others, but also for ourselves. If we start by truly loving and valuing ourselves, then our loving relationship with the world will be built on healthy foundations from which it can grow deep and strong.

Magic

Enchantment ∞ Blessing ∞ Luck ∞ Good Fortune ∞ Synchronicity

Albus says...

I BELIEVE IN FAIRIES, BUT I CAN'T CLAP MY HANDS to save Tinker Bell because I have paws and you'd be surprised how difficult it is to clap with paws. It's difficult not to believe in fairies actually, since they're always chasing me and biting me on the bottom. Sometimes they kiss me on the nose and say sorry and of course I forgive them, since it's all good fun. Fairies like people (and dogs) who have a good sense of humour; and they can bring all kinds of magic into your life. Have they bitten you on the bottom lately? Perhaps soon they'll kiss your nose and bring you something shiny.

Owner's Notes

In our supposedly "rational" society of modern times, most people would claim not to believe in things like magic, but those same people probably still wish each other "good luck," "safe travels," and read their horoscope. The truth is that magic is so deeply woven into all of existence that most people aren't even aware of it.

This card highlights the possibilities of something magical happening in your life, and even if you only glimpse it from the corner of your eye, it's bound to bring you something special.

Magic

FETCH

TASK ∞ MESSAGES ∞ SATISFACTION ∞ REPETITION ∞ RETRIEVAL

Albus says…

Fetch is a great game! You throw the stick; I bring the stick. You throw the stick again; I bring the stick…again! And again and again. It's funny though, because it never gets dull or boring for either of us. Somehow, each time is slightly different and you never know when something unexpected might happen! I've seen humans get very bored and fed up with tasks in their lives that are not so different from playing fetch. Maybe you would enjoy it more if you treated it like a game?

Owner's Notes

Albus is right...again! We all have repetitive tasks in life that we moan about, but maybe we can find the joy and beauty in them instead?

There is satisfaction to be found in jobs well done, and as Albus knows, simple doesn't have to be boring or undesirable! This card may also indicate a delivery or message of some sort, brought on swift paws.

Fetch

Nemesis

Opponent ∞ Conflict ∞ Disruption ∞ Confrontation ∞ Challenge

Albus says...

What? Who? Whhhhy? Even in such a blissful existence as mine, strange and unsettling things can happen. Like cats. One day, you're the sole furry companion in a household and getting all the attention, the next... *Bam!* Cats. Three kittens, to be precise. When things like this happen, it's all about how you handle it. You can be a drama queen and bark your head off all day and sulk all night, and generally make life very difficult for everyone, or you can be nice and friendly and sniff their bottoms and do your best to get on with everyone like I do.

Owner's Notes

We can't all get on with everyone all of the time, sadly. Every so often though, we may find ourselves in a situation that, either because of an individual or certain circumstances, takes us out of our comfort zone. Then, as Albus says, the real test is in how we choose to react. If we react in a negative way or dwell on our perceived misfortune we may well make it worse.

This card may arise when such a test arises, either through a personality clash or through unexpected events. Try to see this challenge as an opportunity for growth, new experience, and who knows, maybe even a new friend?

Cat's Notes

Me iz going to get you. Me iz evil kat. Mwahahahaha…

Nemesis

Resignation

Compromise ∞ Acceptance ∞ Tolerance ∞ Adjustment ∞ Truce

Albus says...

Sigh. Change is inevitable, though it always seems to take us by surprise and it may take a while to get used to! It took me a little while to get used to not being the only furry member of the household anymore, but we soon all learnt to get on together. Mostly that means that I lay here while they run around, jump over me, and climb the curtains.

Resignation

Owner's Notes

We can waste a lot of energy in our lives railing against change, but often, if we stop fighting and accept the change, we can start to see the positive side and accept the lessons it has to offer.

Sometimes the most unexpected things can enhance our lives in unforeseen ways, and once we have accepted them, we wouldn't be without them. Albus and the Catballah Cats are now firm friends, and he actually really enjoys the furry company.

Cat's Notes

When you iz not looking, me iz still going to get you...mwhahahahaha!

Brave

Courage ∞ Curiosity ∞ Initiation ∞ Fears ∞ Strength

Albus says...

Being brave isn't about not being afraid of things; it's about facing our fears. You never really know how brave you are until you have to step into the dark places. Sometimes you have to, though—like if a stick has been thrown down there! You can't just leave a thrown stick down in the darkness; it's just not good dog behaviour. But then when I bring the stick back out of the darkness, it is so exciting and I feel so pleased with myself. I mean there could have been trolls down there, or anything...

Owner's Notes

Sticks do sometimes fall into dark places. What is your equivalent of Albus's stick? Delving into the dark and facing our fears can lead to discovering our true potential. Our most precious treasures are often hidden away, waiting to be uncovered, and when we face the situations or parts of ourselves that make us uncomfortable we have an opportunity to access hidden strengths, talents, and abilities.

We have to decide whether to face our fears or turn away, but if we take the easier option, we deny ourselves access to something truly precious.

Brave

Running

SPEED ∞ MOVEMENT ∞ DIRECTION ∞ FOCUS ∞ LIBERATION

Albus says...

The open space beckons and I can just run and run and run! I can run as fast as the wind when there's nothing to stop me or get in my way. There's no feeling in the world like it! We dogs love to feel the wind in our fur and hear our paws pounding like horse's hooves on the earth. I've seen people run, if they are running to catch a bus, or running away from something. Sometimes you run in races, too. I think you should try just running for the fun of it!

Owner's Notes

It's a joy just watching Albus run, so you can imagine how wonderful it must feel!

If this card comes up for you, it means that nothing can stand in your way, so don't hold back! Put your plans into action, launch yourself forward into a better future, or simply run for the sheer joy of it. If you have somewhere in mind that you are hoping to reach, now is the time.

Running

Roll Over

Appeasement ∞ Obedience ∞ Subservience ∞ Performance ∞ Orders

Albus says…

I am happy to roll over! It's my way of showing you that you're the boss and also a hint that I would like my tummy rubbed. Sometimes, it's a good way of scratching my back. I do my best to make everyone happy, and I know that means that I must do as I'm told. I have my place in the world and it's a good one! I like my tummy rubbed and I'm pretty sure you like to rub it.

Owner's Notes

A good dog knows his place in the world, but it tends to be a lot more complicated for us humans! Power games and status are important to some of us, but there does come a time when we should maybe concede to others and learn how to take orders. After all, we can't all be boss all of the time.

If this card comes up for you, try thinking about your relationship with authority, and whether it's really worthwhile challenging a point or whether it's time to "roll over."

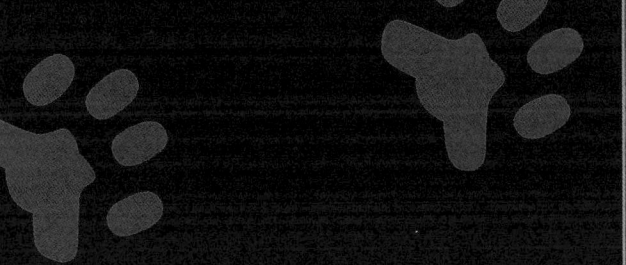

Roll Over

SQUIRREL!

DISTRACTION ∞ SURPRISE ∞ TAUNT ∞ NAUGHTINESS ∞ ANARCHY

Albus says...

SQUIRREL!
Hmmm? Sorry, did you want something?

Owner's Notes

Oh, Albus! You're never going to catch it, you know. Do try to pay attention! All of us have our "Squirrel" moments. You know there's something you're supposed to be doing, but whatever it is flies out of the window as something comes along to distract you. It might be a television program, an individual, or a shiny thing, but whatever it is renders you temporarily entranced and useless for any practical task.

If this card comes up for you, try to focus on whatever it is that really needs your attention, and leave the squirrel to its own business!

Squirrel!

Big Stick

Ambition ∞ Optimism ∞ Strength ∞ Perseverance ∞ Stubborness

Albus says…

People may stop and stare. They may say to me, "Albus, that stick is too big" or "That's more like a tree than a stick!" but I don't listen. Yes, it is a big stick and I like it that way. Why always aim for the little twigs? There's no challenge in a little twig, and it only takes one little bite and it turns all to splinters. Maybe I won't be able to budge this stick far from its spot, but I will have given it a good try, had a good ol' chomp, and I'll be able to say to my friends, "It was *this* big"…

Owner's Notes

If we don't aim high, we're unlikely to achieve great things in life. Albus knows that, though his ambitions don't go much further than a big stick, he puts his whole self behind that stick. I've seen him drag small trees for some distance! We can all learn a lot from his ambitious and determined attitude.

If this card comes up for you, have a think about what your "big stick" is, and how you can achieve anything you put your mind to!

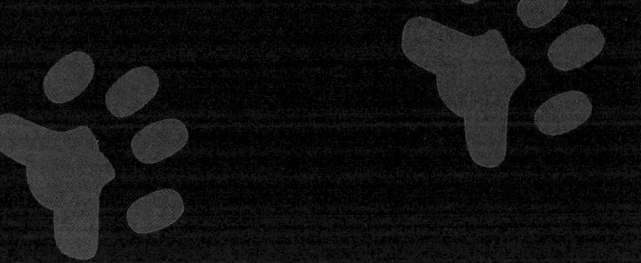

Big Stick

PLAYTIME

ENTERTAINMENT ∞ FRIVOLITY ∞ PLAYFULNESS ∞ ENJOYMENT ∞ CAREFREE

Albus says…

I LOVE TO PLAY! I LOVE TO PLAY WITH OTHER DOGS, or with people, or with my toys, or all three! I'm sure you like to play, too, but people are such funny creatures. They always put work and responsibilities and boring things before playtime, sometimes so much so that they end up with no playtime at all! What kind of life is that? Silly! Play with me?

Owner's Notes

Everyone needs to relax and have a bit of fun now and again. True, we do have responsibilities and work to think of, and that can be very hard for Albus to understand, but we must always make time to be frivolous and carefree sometimes, too. Being able to play as well as work keeps us healthy and in balance. It also helps us to keep life in perspective so that nagging troubles can take a backseat for a while and we can give ourselves permission to enjoy ourselves!

Playtime

LOYALTY

TRUST ∞ KINSHIP ∞ RELIABLE ∞ DEVOTION ∞ BOND

Albus says...

We dogs are known for our loyalty, and it is a wonderful thing indeed when we feel that the devotion runs both ways. To find an owner we can trust as much as they will always be able to trust us, makes a dog feel very lucky indeed. When this true loyalty is found, a strong connection is formed between dog and human that will never be broken.

Owner's Notes

Dogs are indeed extremely loyal creatures and it is a quality we can all aspire to. We should be sure that our devotion to others is returned and not misplaced, as loyalty is a trait that is sadly abused at times.

This card indicates a strong bond of trust, be it between dog and human, human and human, or indeed any pair of beings!

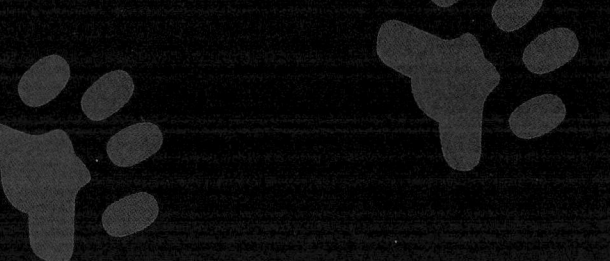

Loyalty

WOLF

DARK SIDE ∞ SHADOW SELF ∞ ANGER ∞ WILD ∞ SUPPRESSION

Albus says...

They say all dogs are wolves under the surface. The same goes for people, too, you know. There is always a wild, shadow self that longs to surface. People find this idea frightening and prefer to keep such things hidden and suppressed, but if it is a part of you, then you are not complete without it. My inner wolf and I are good friends. We have run through the great forest together and he's really not so bad, once you get to know him. He does have an unfortunate habit of chasing sheep though... What does your inner wolf get up to?

Owner's Notes

We do all have an inner wolf, but rather than deny it and keep it buried, we can gain much understanding by acknowledging its presence and power. Indeed, it is only through facing our shadow selves that we can gain proper control and be fully present in our power.

A suppressed and unacknowledged wolf can manifest as an unpredictable temper and will find its own undesirable ways of expressing itself if buried underneath fear and self-doubt.

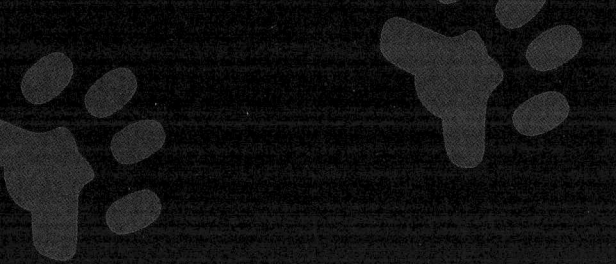

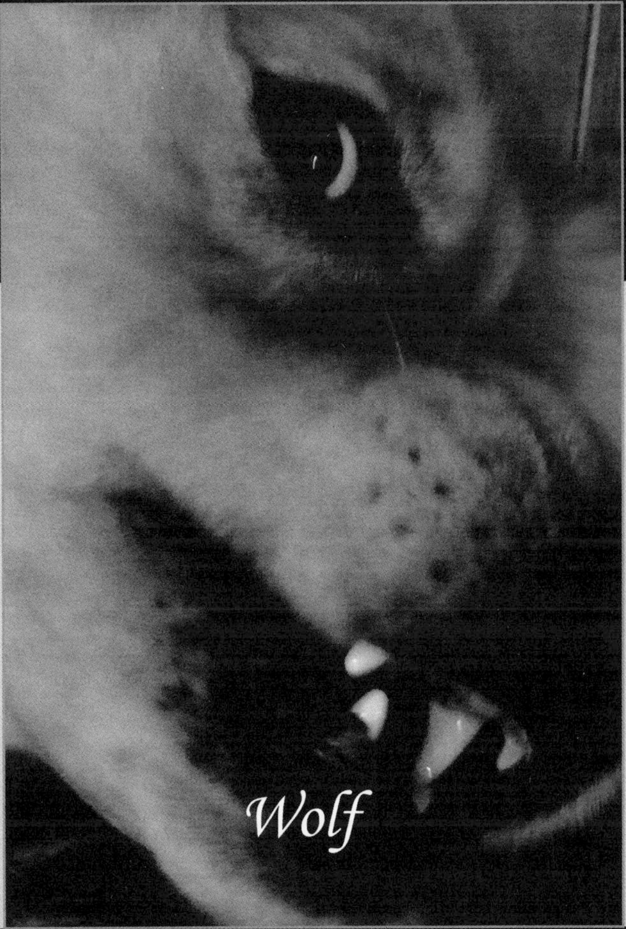

Wolf

ADVENTURE

SPIRIT ∞ PIONEER ∞ RISK ∞ NEW GROUND ∞ EXPERIMENTATION

Albus says…

Ah, the call of the horizon! An adventure beckons! New lands to discover, new sticks to chew and new trees to pee against! I love adventures. You don't even need to go that far, you know. I bet there's a road right by your house you haven't been up yet, or a gap between hedges that you haven't yet passed through… What's stopping you?

Owner's Notes

Adventures feed the soul and keep the spirit young. They can take us to far-flung and exotic lands or, as Albus says, simply through the gap in the hedge we haven't explored yet, but wherever they take us, they always start with that first step out of the door. Even well-trodden paths hold the possibilities of new encounters and magical occurrences.

If this card comes up for you today, be open to new experiences and open your heart to the possibility of adventure. Who knows where that first step out of the door might lead?

Adventure

Good boy

Reputation ∞ Praise ∞ Recognition ∞ Pride ∞ Accolade

Albus says…

I'm a good boy! Being called a good boy is the best thing in the world. I couldn't hope or ask for anything more than being a good boy! Being a good boy means that you value me for everything I am and everything I do for you. It means that you see me, and that I am important to you. I do everything I can to make you happy, and when you call me good boy, I know I have achieved that, and that makes me happy, too…happier than ever!

Owner's Notes

We all need to be acknowledged for hard work. Sometimes, though, we simply need to be acknowledged for who we are and what we mean to those who are important to us.

When this card appears, think about how you can help those around you feel valued. It also may mean that you're due some praise yourself. Well done. Nobody else in the world could do such a good job of being you!

Good Boy

DIVINATION

SINGLE-CARD DRAW

The simplest and most popular use for oracle cards is to draw a single card to give an idea of the day ahead or to bring some understanding and context to the day that is past, and that would certainly be an effective use for this particular deck.

It's important to give the cards a good shuffle whilst focusing on a specific question or in a meditative state. This imbues the cards with your energy, or if you prefer a more scientific reason, enables your subconscious mind to influence the order of the cards according to the information that it is privy to, that your conscious mind is not. Specific questions give more focused answers, and the phrasing of a good question is an art in itself. *Yes* or *No* questions are generally best avoided, as there is not necessarily a distinctively positive or negative message to the cards. Try to form a question that is open to advice; for example, *"What career opportunities should I look out for today?"* instead of *"Will I get the job?"*

To choose your card, find a method that works best for you; there is no set right or wrong way! Once you've shuffled to your satisfaction, you may choose to cut the pack, spread the cards face down on a table, or simply rifle through them face down in your hands until you get to one that you feel drawn to.

Albus Says…

Oh, me, me, me! Let me choose one! You could lay them out on the floor and let your canine companion sniff out your card for the day, or if you wanted to know what was going on in their head, maybe they could pick a card that will tell you? You might be surprised!

Divinatory Spreads

Simple Wisdom of the Household Dog is meant to be just that – simple! However, if you do fancy trying out something slightly more detailed than the single-card draw, Albus has thought up some special doggy divination card spreads for you to try…

The Stick

Albus's version of the simplest card spread, "The Stick," shows us where the stick was thrown from, what may be encountered whilst chasing the stick, and where the stick will land. In other words, it shows where you have been, where you are now, and where you are going—or past, present, and future. It may help to bring some detail and context to the reading if you can decide what your "stick" is. Could it be a relationship? An ambition? A creative project?

1- The Throw

The stick is thrown and a chain of events is set into motion… This card highlights a key moment in your recent past that has led to where you are right now.

2- The Chase

The present is a moment in time that is constantly moving, just like Albus chasing the stick! This card shows you where you are at the moment and what direction you are heading in your pursuit of the stick.

3- The Discovery

Finally, the stick is in your grasp…or is it? Was this the stick you were looking for, or a different stick? It may be a better stick, or it may be a soggy twig. This card shows you where your current chase will lead you, but of course no chase ever *really* ends…

Paws for Thought

Here's a slightly more complex spread from Albus, obviously inspired by his own pawprint! This spread is designed to look at the different parts of yourself and aspects of your life to see whether they are in harmony or if there is any imbalance, and if so, where that imbalance may lie.

Albus Says…

I was contemplating my paw, and I noticed that although really it is one thing, it is made up of different bits. That made me think about how people and dogs are all made out of different bits, too. I'm not talking about legs and tails and heads and bottoms, but I mean the things that make us who we are inside.

1- In the central position

This card represents the whole self as you appear to the world.

2- The second card position

Represents the workings of your mind, recurring thoughts and your mental health.

3- The third card position

Represents your physical existence, your health, and your finances.

4- The fourth card position

Connection to your emotional life, friendships, and romantic relationships.

5- The fifth card position

Relates to creative ideas, activities, inspiration, as well as the spiritual side of your existence.

Meat on the Bone

Albus loves a good meaty bone, just like we people enjoy a good meaty opportunity. If you have an opportunity arise in your life, but you want to be sure of the pros and cons, this is a great spread to use to gain some clarity.

Albus Says...

Mmmmm...boooone

1- THE FIRST CARD

Place horizontally in the centre. It represents the nature of the opportunity itself.

2- THE SECOND CARD

Place above and to the left, (see illustration). It represents something positive that may have to be left behind in order to take full advantage of the opportunity.

3- THE THIRD CARD

Place below the second card. It represents something negative that must be left behind.

4- THE FOURTH CARD

Place above and to the right. It represents a positive change that will be generated by the opportunity.

5- THE FIFTH CARD

Place below the fourth card. It represents the possible disadvantages of embracing the opportunity.

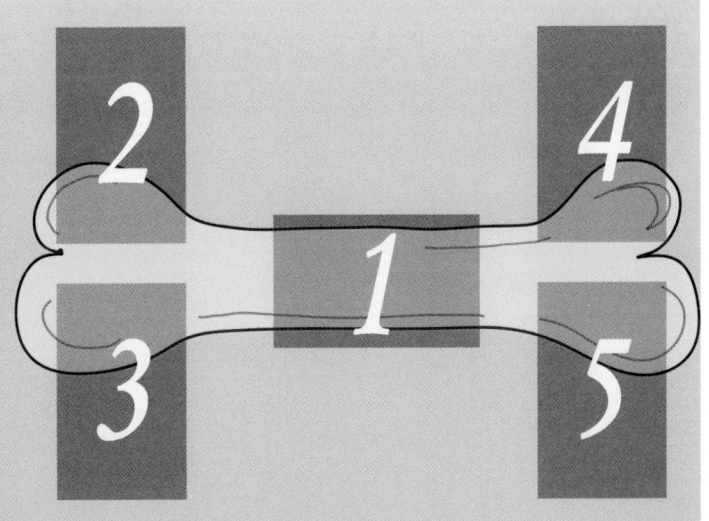

I hope you've enjoyed this insight into the *Simple Wisdom of the Household Dog*, and that you will continue to enjoy these cards for years to come. Remember these insights when life starts to bog you down. At least they might make you smile, an ability which should never be underrated. At best, they may part the clouds that sometimes obscure the light of truth. May they become a loyal companion to you in the days and years to come, just as Albus is to me.

Albus Says…

ARE WE FINISHED? CAN WE GO FOR WALKIES NOW? HOORAY! I LOVE YOU!

Albus Dumbledog is a three and a half year old Golden Retriever. He lives with his human pack members in a converted chapel in beautiful, muddy Cornwall, where he never wants for sticks, walkies, or treats. Albus likes to eat, go for walks, and roll in smelly stuff. This is Albus's first creative project and he found the typing quite difficult with his big dumbley paws. Although he had to get one of his humans to help with the writing and photography, the wisdom is all his.

Emily Carding is an artist and author and, of course, Albus's owner! She has created a number of popular Tarot and Oracle decks, including the *The Transparent Tarot, The Transparent Oracle,* and *Tarot of the Sidhe* for Schiffer Publishing, LTD. She is also the author of *Faery Craft,* (Llewellyn, 2012) and the illustrator of *Gods of the Vikings* by Marion Pearce, (Avalonia, 2010). She has contributed essays and cover images for a number of anthologies for Avalonia Books and is currently working on a number of exciting new projects. To keep up to date with Emily's work, please visit www.childofavalon.com.